— Monica,
One last word.....

Always appreciate your
power to be kind and nice.
You have it. Thank you
for being you.
Fondly,
Clare

My thanks over
and over —

Kindness Grows

Real Stories About Random Acts of Kindness

BARB WALTERS

BALBOA.
PRESS
A DIVISION OF HAY HOUSE

Balboa Press books may be ordered through booksellers or by contacting:

Balboa Press
A Division of Hay House
1663 Liberty Drive
Bloomington, IN 47403
www.balboapress.com
1 (877) 407-4847

Because of the dynamic nature of the Internet, any web addresses or
links contained in this book may have changed since publication and
may no longer be valid. The views expressed in this work are solely those
of the author and do not necessarily reflect the views of the publisher,
and the publisher hereby disclaims any responsibility for them.

The author of this book does not dispense medical advice or prescribe the use
of any technique as a form of treatment for physical, emotional, or medical
problems without the advice of a physician, either directly or indirectly. The
intent of the author is only to offer information of a general nature to help
you in your quest for emotional and spiritual well-being. In the event you use
any of the information in this book for yourself, which is your constitutional
right, the author and the publisher assume no responsibility for your actions.

Any people depicted in stock imagery provided by Thinkstock are
models, and such images are being used for illustrative purposes only.
Certain stock imagery © Thinkstock.

Printed in the United States of America.

ISBN: 978-1-4525-8791-2 (sc)
ISBN: 978-1-4525-8792-9 (e)
Library of Congress Control Number: 2013921760

Balboa Press rev. date: 3/21/2014

Acknowledgments

I would like to express my great appreciation to Alice Sharp for her bird illustrations and editorial guidance. She encouraged me to listen to the critique and suggestions of others, but she reminded me that this was in fact *my* book. That kind advice helped me immensely, and it made the process easier.

I would like to offer my special thanks to Alyssa Reinert Wassmer for artfully creating the hands and flower image I requested. I am lucky to have such a talented friend!

I am incredibly fortunate to have had the assistance given by Everything Printing with my files and manuscript. Kevin Rhude deserves special thanks and praise. As a new author, I was very inexperienced, but I always felt comfortable asking for guidance. Working with Everything Printing was a positive experience, and I appreciate all of their help.

My husband and daughter supported me through all of the challenges of completing this book. Thank you for your encouragement and for understanding how important it was to me. You gave me two of my favorite reviews when you told me that the book made you feel good, and that others will want to read it!

I would like to thank my dad for his continued interest and excitement about the book. He really helped motivate me to try something new and make it happen. Thank you for always believing in me dad!

I am particularly grateful for the assistance given by my story contributors. Each story shines like a beam of light, making the world just a little bit brighter. The stories emphasize the importance of human connection and being present. You all helped make my book a reality, and I am forever grateful that our paths have crossed in such a positive way! Thank you so much for your enthusiasm, caring, sharing, and believing in the power of random acts of kindness!

Sharing Your Kindness

You know that feeling you get when you surprise someone with an act of kindness? What about the last time someone was unexpectedly kind to you? Whether you are the giver, or the receiver, you feel a spark. That feeling, that spark, is at the root of random acts of kindness. Random acts of kindness are those moments when we are motivated to make someone happy. We want to make their life

easier. These selfless acts brighten and lift up another. They can happen spontaneously, or they can be planned. These acts can come out of sad events, frustrating situations, or just old-fashioned good will. We can give in a way that is not a common, everyday occurrence. The idea of giving and expecting nothing in return is at the heart of random acts of kindness. We give out of caring or compassion, not because we have to.

There are opportunities every day to be kind. When we make mindful connections we are aware, and we are in the moment. We are willing to take a risk. Start a conversation with an elderly person in a store. You may be the only person he or she speaks to all day. Let someone ahead of you in line. Pay the toll of the driver behind you at the tollbooth. Acknowledge something that someone has done for you. Send somebody a card, or a handwritten note. Sometimes the kindest thing that you can do for another person is to just listen to him.

People do not even realize that they have the cognition to change their routine and look at situations in a different way. If you step outside of your normal routine just a little bit, it can change the way you react to situations. Focus on your ability to positively connect with others. The results can be rewarding. Random acts of kindness do not have to be big productions, but their results can be huge. Sometimes a small thing that you do for someone can end up changing his or her life. It would be great if we could make a conscious effort every day to be aware of our surroundings and help someone in some way. When we get into the habit of doing this, more and more opportunities to perform acts of kindness come to the surface. We become energized, and our mood gets a boost. When we see positive results, we gain the confidence to reach out and help others more often. It feels great to do some small thing that ends up making someone's day.

It seems like many people are walking around in their own worlds. Some do not even look up from their cell phones. This is sad. We are so "connected" that we may be losing some connection on a personal level. Social media really is a miraculous way to communicate with people all over the world. It is different though. Somehow, communicating electronically can leave us feeling hollow. We miss the body language, the voice inflection, and the closeness of human interaction. One on one human connection can be better for the heart. It feels more solid, and more real.

Life can be very challenging. If you listen to the news, it can be overwhelming, due to the economy, unemployment, healthcare, wars, catastrophes. There is up-to-the-minute access to every bad thing that happens in the world. It is easy to feel bombarded with the negative information. This can lead to feeling depressed, anxious or even hopeless. When you feel this way, do something nice for somebody. You will feel better. When you get in the habit of finding ways to be kind, you can change the way you think about your life.

We are trained to focus on what is not working in our world, our community, or ourselves. Find out what *is* working for you. Find it, focus on what makes you happy, and share it. If you take a moment and think about the positive aspects in yourself, and in your life, you will become more grateful. When you reach out to someone in need, you become more grateful for the abundance in your own life. Sometimes we take that for granted. Listen to your inner voice. Go with your intuition. When you serve others, the light comes back into your life. You feel brighter and energized. It does not matter who you are, where you live, or how old you are. We all have something to offer. When we share it, well, that is the big picture. That is where kindness fits in.

Being kind does not make you weak or a pushover. Some people may look at kindness as a soft issue in the grand scheme of things, but being kind takes courage. It takes confidence and it involves taking a chance. When you carry out acts of kindness, you will be doing important things with your life. You will be a powerful person. Kindness can deliver what you need most from your life. Kindness is like good karma. The goodness always comes back to you in some way, shape, or form. When you put kindness out into the universe, you will help someone. They will pass it on, and help someone in return. Kindness will keep growing and growing, with no end. Share your kindness with the world, and see what happens!

Harry

I was driving home from a day of shopping. As I was coming around the bend of the road, I noticed a little gentleman who had to be in his mid-70's. He was nicely dressed in a yellow shirt and dress pants, but what really stood out was that he was standing on his tiptoes with this right thumb straight up in the air. He had a look of urgency on his face. I stopped and asked him if he needed any help. I thought he had broken down somewhere.

He looked serious and yelled over to me, "Can you take me to the tavern down the road?" I was not expecting that, and I cracked up and told him to get in. I had never picked up a hitchhiker before, but somehow today was different. I asked him to put on his seatbelt, and as he fastened the seat belt he said, "Hi! I'm Harry! Don't worry. I'm not a criminal. I just felt like a cold one!" Harry told me a lot about himself. He was originally from New Orleans, he was in good health, and his mother lived to be 99. He was quite a pleasant, upbeat person. He had great energy, and I really enjoyed our brief time together. Harry said that he was unable to drive his vehicle at this time, and that is why he counts on the kindness of strangers.

As I pulled into the parking lot, I asked Harry if he was going to sit outside on the deck and watch the Phillies game, and he smiled and nodded. I told him that maybe my husband and I would see him in the tavern sometime. Harry looked up at the sky and stared for a few seconds, smiled, and then he let out a big sigh. He said it was such a beautiful day, and he thanked me for making it even better.

As he was getting out of the car, he poked his head back in, and in his happy-go-lucky manner, he reminded me that every act of kindness is always returned. I drove away from the tavern, and I smiled thinking about Harry. I looked up at the sky. It really was a beautiful day.

> *"Kindness, like a boomerang, always returns."*
> -Author Unknown

Work with Me

I work for - I mean *with* - a really cool woman who has taught me a lot about people and about life. One day I told her that it was a real pleasure to work for her, and she got very serious. She said, "Let me explain something to you. I want to be very clear: You do not work *for* me. You work *with* me."

> *"A good character is the best tombstone. Those who loved you and were helped by you will remember you when forget-me-nots have withered. Carve your name on hearts, not on marble."*
> - Charles H. Spurgeon

Every Person Has A Story

*S*pring was finally here and it was the first sunny Saturday in ages. I drove to the park, and I took a nice walk along the river. The sunshine was quite deceiving because it was still quite chilly outside. The wind was strong and blowing in my face, so I decided to cut the walk a little short. As I drove home, I noticed many people walking and holding bags. I stopped at a store and on my way back to my car, I noticed more people walking and carrying bags. I realized that these people were walking from the closest grocery store that was a mile away. I knew they had to cross a six-lane highway to get to where I now sat in my car. The closest houses or apartments were at least another mile away. I started my car and drove towards the exit.

A couple in their 30's had walked in front of my car and as I watched them pass, I noticed the woman was having difficulty walking, and she was struggling with her groceries. I put down my passenger window and yelled for them, but they did not hear me through the wind. I beeped my horn and waved to them, "Would you like a ride?" I yelled. The woman touched the man's arm and told him that they had a ride. They both got in with six bags of groceries.

"Thank you so much! Praise the Lord, you are an angel!" she said. I asked them where they needed to go and I started driving. They each thanked me about five times. Then the woman said something that touched me so much I could feel it in my heart. She said, "My leg is really bad and I'm always supposed to use my cane. That cane really gets in the way when I carry groceries, so I left it behind today. My leg hurts so badly. You don't know how much this means to us." The man said, "We have to eat so we just do what we can. We will never forget your kindness."

As I pulled into the parking lot of their apartment building, I asked them if I could help them carry in their groceries. They refused my offer, and said that I had done enough already. I watched them walk towards the building. The man was carrying five of the bags and the woman was carrying one. She was walking with great difficulty from side to side. I noticed the same walk outside the store. I assumed that she was struggling because of the heavy groceries and strong winds. If I had not given them a ride that day I never would have discovered the real reason that she was having such a tough time walking. She left her cane at home so she could carry her groceries.

> "Give a gift of a smile, Give a gift of a hug, Give
> a gift of a helping hand . . . and you give a gift
> from the heart that is priceless."
> - Mattie J.T. Stepanek

Mountain Road

My husband and I were driving to a state park in the mountains. We were traveling on a hilly, winding road. Around the bend, sat a van parked sideways, nearly covering both lanes of traffic. A very old, very skinny hand reached out the driver's window, waving us by. We slowly drove alongside the van, and an elderly woman inside asked if we could help her. She told us her hip was broken, and she needed help to her house on the hill. She pointed to the house, and there were at least 60 steps leading up to the house on a hill nearby.

The whole thing was very strange, and we were uneasy. Was she a decoy, and were we being set up to be robbed? Was anyone hiding in the van? How can you drive with a broken hip? We had a lot of questions! We looked at her, and we looked at each other. We decided that we had to help her. We pulled over to the edge of the road, and she did the same. Cautiously, we approach the van, and discovered that she was alone. She had a bunch of groceries in the back, and she told me to grab the groceries as my husband helped her out of the van and up each step to her house.

I got quite a shock when I got to the top of the steps with the groceries. The old woman had already put my husband to work, and I watched in disbelief as she instructed him as he put down mousetraps for her! I asked if there were any other chores to do, and I inquired about her situation. She informed me that she was recuperating from a broken hip and that she had someone to help her to her van and someone else helped her at the grocery store. She just needed more help once she got home. I was stunned that she was waiting by the road for any random person to assist her. She told us that we were angels, and that car after car just drove by. She thanked us and told us how grateful she was for stopping and helping her.

"Each person has inside a basic decency and goodness. If he listens to it and acts on it, he is giving a great deal of what it is to the world needs most. It is not complicated, but it takes courage. It takes courage for a person to listen to his own goodness and act on it."

-Pablo Casals

Thank You

A wise and generous friend gave me a very nice gift. I started to say that he shouldn't have and that it was too much, but he stopped me and gave me the same advice that was given to him by a wise and generous friend: *When someone gives you a gift, it is because they want to.*

If the receiver says they do not deserve it or it is too much it makes everyone uncomfortable. He told me that it takes practice, but over time it will get easier. Just look the person directly in the eye and say *thank you*.

"Whatever you give, that's what you receive, nothing more. This is the law of nature."
- Swami Muktananda

Growing Up

*I*t was May 1947, Philadelphia PA. I was a senior at Central High School, an all-boys school in the city. We were two weeks away from traveling to Washington DC for our senior class trip. We were all excited about the idea of leaving home and exploring another city. We all realized that this would be the last time that we would be together as a group with the exception of graduation. We were meeting in the auditorium to review the itinerary of our trip. One of the teachers stood up and said, "Guys, I have some bad news. Two of the hotels that we are staying in will not allow our black students to stay there." Unbelievably, in 1947, Washington DC was a segregated city. There were 20 black students in our class of 250.

Many students loudly voiced their disapproval: "Boo! That's not right!" One of the students shouted, "Let's cancel the trip!" Our teacher said that this was an option. He told us that there was no way we could find another hotel for all of us in less than two weeks. "We will take a vote," he announced. "How many of you think that we should cancel the trip?" Without hesitation, every single student raised his hand. All 250 students unanimously voted against the trip. The decision was swift and exhilarating. I looked over at one of my black friends and he looked proud. I felt the same way. It was a very grown-up decision. We were saying a lot about our values and our integrity. We chose to support an issue that was bigger than our own desires. I am sure that we would have had a great time if we had gone to DC, but nothing could compare to that feeling we all had when we took that vote.

"When I was younger I thought success was something different. I thought when I grow up I want to be famous. I want to be a star. I want to be in movies. When I grow up, I want to see the world and drive nice cars. I want to have groupies. But my idea of success is different today. For me the most important thing in your life is to live your life with integrity and not give in to peer pressure and try to be something you're not. To live your life as an honest and compassionate person, to contribute in some way."

- Ellen DeGeneres, 2009 Tulane
Commencement Speech

Brownies

I was a Brownie in the Girl Scouts when I was a kid. My mom was a cookie mother. I remember a large part of our downstairs covered with boxes of Girl Scout cookies, and the Brownies helped sell them too. I remember selling the cookies door-to-door. It was fun, but the cookie mother had a lot of work. She had to be very organized and patient.

Recently I was in a grocery store that was shutting down permanently. The shelves were not fully stocked, and there was very little foot traffic. There was a table set up with Girl Scout cookies by one of the doors. There were three Brownies about nine years old with a woman. I assumed she was the mother of one of the girls. I watched people walk by and ignore the girls; though I saw the girls smile and try to get the attention of the shoppers. They seemed hopeful but they were being rejected.

I walked up to their table and asked them how business was. They smiled and asked me if I would like to buy any cookies. I told them that I had to have a box of the Thin Mints. I also mentioned that I used to be a Brownie, and selling cookies was hard work. They must have gotten up early and they may have encountered some unfriendly people. I told them that I really like their attitude, and to keep trying and keep smiling. I handed them $20 for the $3 box, and I wished them luck. The girls squealed with delight and the mother mouthed, "Thank you."

> *"If you want others to be happy, practice compassion. If you want to be happy, practice compassion."*
>   - Dalai Lama

Champagne and Caviar

My wife and I live in an apartment that is attached to a beautiful old farmhouse. We have a wonderful view of acres of fields. One day we were watching TV when we heard an odd noise outside. We went out and saw a huge colorful hot air balloon and it looked like it was about to land in our field! We walked down the lane towards the field and the balloon nimbly landed right in the middle. The people inside the basket were having a lot of fun. They yelled and waved for us to come over.

When we got there, they handed us glasses of champagne and caviar with crackers. We stood there toasting each other. I couldn't believe that five minutes ago my wife and I were watching TV. Now we were drinking champagne and eating caviar in the middle of our field with complete strangers!

> *"A bit of fragrance always clings to the hand that gives roses."*
>
> > - Chinese proverb

Bermuda

When I was nine, my family went on a vacation to Bermuda. I did not know it at the time, but this would be our last vacation as a family, since my mother was at the end stages of cancer. She used a walker, and she was very thin and frail. A cab picked us up at the airport, and my dad asked the driver to take us to the villa where we were staying. The driver asked us if we would like to take a more scenic route. We eagerly agreed. We saw tropical flowers, pastel colored homes, and stunning old buildings in pristine condition. All the people of Bermuda wore bright, colorful clothing, and they smiled and waved as we drove past. The beaches really do have pink sand! This country was so clean and beautiful. I loved it already!

When we arrived at our villa, my dad and the cab driver helped my mother out of the cab. We had been sightseeing for an extra 45 minutes at least. I heard my dad ask the driver how much he owed him. The driver refused to take any payment. My dad was getting a little upset, especially since the driver had given us this special tour. My dad insisted on paying, but the cab driver pleaded with my dad to let him do this.

I will never forget what I saw when I turned around and looked at them. My dad and the cab driver were shaking hands for what seemed like a long time, and their eyes were locked. I stared at them, and I knew that they were saying so much to each other without even saying a word.

> *"Kindness makes a fellow feel good whether it's done to him or by him."* -Frank Howard Clark

More Than Money

I have my own cleaning business. I have had several clients for many years, and we are friends and discuss problems as any friend would. One day I was talking about an outrageous medical bill. Since I am self-employed, I have my own health insurance. I have opted for a large deductible. I was upset about how high my deductible is, and that I owed so much. So I was venting.

The woman I work for turned to me without hesitation and said, "Would you like $1000?" I was stunned. This was not a loan. She was sincerely offering. Although I did not take her up on her offer, the fact that she made the offer meant more to me than the thousand dollars. A lot more.

> *"Kindness is the greatest wisdom."*
>
> -Author Unknown

Special

I stopped at a local coffee shop, and I ordered a small coffee at the drive-through window. The woman told me to pull around. I got my money ready and I put down my window. There was a young woman at the window with a big smile on her face. She handed me my coffee at the same time I handed her the money. She told me not to pay today, and I asked her why not. She said, "You're special!" She gave me a big smile and a thumbs-up sign. "I am?" I asked. She nodded and gave me the thumbs- up again. I smiled and drove away. I didn't know what was making me feel so good. Was it the free coffee, or could it have been what she said?

I got to work and said to my friend, "Hey Jenn, I'm special!" I told her what happened and she smiled and said, "You are special!" The next time I saw my friend she said that she had something really funny to tell me. Apparently, the coffee shop was having a promotion of a free small coffee on the day that I got my coffee. All the small coffees were free! I thought about it, and I could not get over what a genius that young woman was. Instead of telling people the coffee is free and everyone gets one, she tells people that they are special, smiles and gives a thumbs- up sign. What a great life lesson! After all, how often are we told that we are special?

> "The true meaning of life is to plant trees, under
> whose shade you do not expect to sit."
> - Nelson Henderson

That Note

I knew a girl at school who was picked on relentlessly and she never defended herself. She had very little self-esteem and few friends. I would stick up for her in class and on the bus. I wanted to let her know that we were friends. She told me she was going to be cyber-schooled after middle school. It was a smart move; I don't think she could've handled high school. On the last day of middle school, I handed her a note. In it, I said that she was a good friend and a great person. I wished her luck and hoped to see her this summer. I watched her read it, and she started to cry.

When I got on the bus, I saw her sitting with her head down. I was concerned, but when I got closer I realized that she was sitting there staring at that note.

> "The greatest good you can do for another is not just share your riches, but to reveal to him his own."
>
> - Benjamin Disraeli

Keep On Truckin'

I was driving back to college on a major highway in central PA. I was halfway there with another hour and a half to go, when I got a flat tire. I never had a flat tire before. It was 90 degrees out and I didn't even want to get out of my car, because cars and trucks were flying by so fast. I was scared, and I did not know what to do.

Suddenly, an 18-wheeler pulled up in front of me, and a very large man got out. I got out of my passenger-side door to talk to him as we both looked at my tire. He said that the tire was flat but it might be able to be repaired. He looked at my spare and it wasn't good. It definitely would not make the hour and a half trip back to school. He said he could take my tire to a service station to get it fixed. I told him I'd stay with my car, and he said his truck had AC and it could be a while. I figured this was my best option, and we headed for the truck.

As I was climbing into the truck, I was getting nervous. I couldn't believe that I was getting into a stranger's tractor-trailer! When I got into the seat I saw a cross hanging from the rearview mirror on a chain which made me feel a little better. I sure hoped this man was as kind as he seemed. When we got to the service station, I was relieved that some of the workers knew him. He was gone for a while. When he returned he told me that it was taken care of and we drove all the way back to my car. After he put the tire on my car, I told him that it looked like a brand-new tire, and he said that the other tire couldn't be fixed. I really needed to pay him for the tire and his time, but I only had $12 on me. I asked him if I could mail him a check for the difference plus his time.

The trucker told me that some days he drives for many hours and does not speak to a soul. If in his travels, he can help someone along the way, that it is a good day. He took the $12 and said, "Drive safe now."

> *"Anyone in a state of seeking can never be happy.*
> *Only those who are constantly finding are fulfilled.*
> *And finding is not something that happens to us...*
> *it is something we do."*
>
> -Alan Cohen

Meat Market

Years ago a man in our town owned a bar, which was right next to the grocery store that our family frequented. He would come in to the grocery store a couple of times a week. He'd watch the old ladies, primarily widows, shop. They would pick up a piece of meat, look at the price and put it down. They would usually settle for something much cheaper. He would wait until they passed down the aisle, and then he'd gather up the items the ladies wanted. He took the items to the register and paid for them. He would point the women out to the store clerks to make sure they received their desired items.

> *"If you haven't charity in your heart, you have the*
> *worst kind of heart trouble."*
>
> - Bob Hope

Summertime

*S*ummertime is a time for sharing. My neighbors have a wonderful vegetable and herb garden which they share with my family. We get to pick whatever we like anytime we want several times during the summer. They even plant basil and jalapeno peppers just for me! They leave beautiful fresh vegetables at our door, and I love to repay them with a homemade meal straight from their garden!

> *"The only gift is a portion of thyself... The poet*
> *brings his poem, the painter, his picture; the girl,*
> *a handkerchief of her own sewing."*
>   -Ralph Waldo Emerson, from *Gifts*

Wildflowers

*M*y neighbor takes her dog for long walks in local fields. I envy the fact that she is able to spend so much free time outside enjoying nature. She rang my doorbell one day. I opened the door and she was standing there with her dog on a leash in one hand. With the other hand, she presented me with a big, beautiful bouquet of purple wildflowers.

> *"Let the beauty we love be what we do."*
>   -Rumi

A family of nine lived in my old neighborhood. The father was retired and his wife was a reserved woman who rarely spoke to the neighbors. One of their children was a boy named Melvin. He was close in age to me. He was mentally challenged and he had some physical limitations. Nobody in the neighborhood ever played with him, and he was always alone. A couple of times a week, a boy in the neighborhood would see Melvin outside his house, and he decided to go over and talk to him. He would try to play with him and communicate with him.

Years later Melvin's mother waved down my mother and sister on the street. She told them about the boy who would come over and spend time with Melvin. She mentioned how much it meant to her family, especially her son. She said that she doubted Melvin could have survived all those years had it not been for that boy who decided to reach out and befriend her son. I'm so happy that I was the boy who made a difference in Melvin's life.

> *"To give and then not feel that one has given is the very best of all ways of giving."*
>
> -Max Beerbohm

Teacher

ometimes we are lucky enough to experience a great teacher. I mean a really, exceptional person who not only teaches the 3 R's, but also teaches lessons in life as well. My daughter was fortunate to have such a teacher in elementary school. He had been teaching for thirty years. Many teachers were burned out after that time span, but not this man. He was full of positive energy, and he energized the entire classroom. When he taught the multiplication tables, he would recite them as he jumped rope. If the students followed his lead, and did it correctly, he gave them money! He was paying them coins, and they were jumping rope, laughing, having fun, and learning. Brilliant! The entire school loved this teacher.

My child stopped wanting to go to school and I knew something was wrong. She finally admitted that an older boy in school was picking on her daily. My daughter is a shy, sweet girl, and this boy was very cruel to her. I talked to her teacher about it, and I could tell that he was very upset. He assured me that he would take care of it.

The next day at school, he called my daughter and the boy into his classroom during recess. This nice, pleasant teacher was surprising this kid. Not only was he completely serious, he was angry. He was not playing today. He asked the boy if he liked being called names. He asked him if he believed the things he was saying about my daughter. Then he asked this boy if he was sorry. He made him apologize to my daughter, and she said that when he did, he was crying. I asked my daughter how she felt about it, and she said that he deserved it. She was very calm and content.

She handed me a folded up piece of paper. It was a handwritten letter of apology addressed to my husband and me. My daughter smiled and said that she had one too. As I read the note, I knew that the bullying incident was history. I also knew that this man had a special gift. That gift was teaching.

> "To cultivate kindness is a valuable part of the business of life."
>
> -Samuel Johnson

Sick Day

I am a private contractor and schedule many different customers during my workweek. Some jobs take an hour or two and some take much longer. I received a phone call from a customer where I was planning to spend most of the day. She was canceling because she was sick, and she did not want me to catch whatever she was coming down with. I appreciated her concern for my health, but I couldn't afford to lose a day's pay.

Just before she hung up, she told me that she was still paying me. She also said I should take the day off and do something nice for myself.

> "It's unfortunate and I really wish I wouldn't have to say this, but I really like human beings who have suffered. They're kinder."
>
> - Emma Thompson

Makeover

I am a nurse practitioner at a hospital. I have a small office with a desk. When I took the position, I took the office as is. I had been meaning to spruce it up, but I never got around to it. I told one of the doctors that my office looked very dull. I had a meeting one morning and I wanted to drop my purse off at my desk. I walked into my office, and I put my purse down. I looked up slowly, and I stood there and stared. This was not my office. Everything in there was different and new. It was colorful, organized, and functional. There were pictures on the walls and many special touches. It was beautiful! I had no idea what happened here. I went into the hallway and looked at my coworkers' offices and they were unchanged. I was very confused and I felt disoriented. I thought I was having a medical issue! A doctor and a coworker came over, and they were laughing at my priceless reaction. To my astonishment, that doctor had come in over the weekend and he gave my office a makeover!

> "It's nice to be important but it's more important to be nice."
>
> -Author unknown

Moving

My brother and his wife are both mechanical engineers. They were promoted to new positions in their company. They needed to move from Texas to Malaysia as soon as they sold their house. Their company was motivating them with a large bonus if their house sold quickly. Everyone was thrilled when the house sold in a month.

My brother and his wife stopped and visited my parents and me before they left for their big trip to their new lives so far away. My brother handed my dad a shoebox. My dad took the lid off the shoe box, and I will never forget the look of astonishment on his face! Inside he found receipt after receipt stamped *Paid in full*. Somehow, my brother managed to track down the numerous creditors that my family owed for years. He paid thousands and thousands of dollars- every single credit card bill we owed! My dad was speechless, and to this day, he shakes his head about it, as if it was the nicest thing ever.

> *"Life is not recognized by living as much as it is by giving."*
>
> -Sasha Azevedo

Bright Spot

I was having one of those weeks where nothing was going right. Two major appliances at home broke down, someone close to me really let me down, and I was working extra hours for the past month. I was exhausted and grumpy. Unexpectedly, a friend of mine presented me with a beautiful lined outdoor vest. It was reversible, black on one side and soft leopard print on the other. I loved it! The cooler days were approaching, and I had recently tried one on, but I did not purchase it. Now, here was the perfect vest for me, hand delivered by my friend!

She reminded me that I had complimented her on the one she wore last year. She said that she was happy when she found this one for me, because she knew how much I would like it. She seemed as excited as I was. It just goes to show you, that no matter how bad a time you are having, there will always be a bright spot. The bright spots come more frequently when you have wonderful friends.

> *"Kindness is like snow. It beautifies everything it covers."*
>
> -Samuel Taylor Coleridge

Rosemary

My mother died of cancer when I was ten. It was a very difficult time for my family and me. A few days after the funeral, I returned to school. It was right after the holiday break, and I was not sure how people would act towards me. Some acted very sad and others just looked at me. Many would not make eye contact and everyone seemed awkward around me.

I had a new teacher who was filling in for my teacher who was on maternity leave. I didn't know this teacher and she didn't know me. She had a slight southern accent. She introduced herself to me as Mrs. Robertson, and I told her my name. She looked at me with a big smile and said, "You are just the prettiest little thing! You look just like my niece Rosemary with those pretty eyes!" I smiled and she asked, "Is it okay with you if I call you Rosemary?" I agreed and took it as a compliment. That teacher called me Rosemary for the next few months, and every time she said Rosemary, I felt special. She knew about my mother's death but whenever she saw me, she had a big smile on her face. She would say, "There's my Rosemary." She made me feel like I could make someone smile. She made me feel good. That small act was what I needed. When I think about it today, it still touches my heart.

> "Sometimes someone says something really small
> and it fits into this empty space in your heart."
> - From the TV show *My So-called Life*

25

Change Your World

I was 19, working two jobs, and taking college classes in the city. I was lonely, hungry and despondent. My parents were divorced and growing up in my family was a complete disaster. There was a lot of abuse, and I did not think that I could ever overcome it all. I felt like my life would always be dysfunctional, and I began to wonder if life was worth living any more.

One day in a busy food court, I was counting my money to see if I had enough to buy something to eat, since I needed most of it for the train ride home. I looked up and saw a very tall, well-built man wearing a cowboy hat and a trench coat. When he came through the entrance, I noticed his face looked old and it did not match his body. I must have been staring, so he asked me how I was. I felt a strange connection to him, and I told him how tired, broken, and unhappy I was. I couldn't help it, my feelings came flooding out.

He began telling me his story. He was from the Midwest, and his wife and four children were killed in a freak accident. Even after this tragedy, whenever anyone asks how he is doing, his reply is always the same, 'I'm great!' He said that after the ninth or tenth time the positive energy takes over and he really does feel great. He told me that a positive attitude can change your world. It lifts up everyone you meet. This can make you feel great and your positive attitude will have a ripple effect on others. At that point, he took my hands and said, "You are the power in your world. You are in charge of your own happiness, and because of this you can help others!"

Things were starting to click in my head and I was feeling my body changing. It was like pouring soda into a glass. I felt like all the cells of my body were popping and changing. I was waking up! It felt like he was answering a question that I had about my life, but I never knew how to ask. My head was spinning and I turned away from him for a second. When I turned back, the man was gone. I looked all around, but he had vanished. I am completely convinced that he was my angel. He saved me. He helped me change the way I think, and that changed my life.

> "We do not sing because we are happy. We are happy because we sing."
>> - William James

Angel

If you are lucky, you might spot a living angel in my town. She passes out dollar bills to children, and she watches their faces light up. This small gesture becomes a moment to remember for these children and their parents. The woman wishes to remain anonymous. She just wants to show her love for children, and it makes them happy. She is restoring my faith in humanity.

> "Light of the world, shine on me, love is the answer."
>> - Todd Rundgren

Mourning

My cat had been sick for a month, and she was not responding to the medication. Just before I went into work, I phoned my husband from my car. I wanted to see how she was. I could hear it in his voice that she died. I sat in my car, and I cried longer and harder than I have cried in years. She meant so much to our family and we loved her. After composing myself, I walked into work. My boss asked me how I was. I tried to keep it together, but I burst into tears. I told him that my cat died, and I just found out. I assured him that I would be fine in a few minutes. He told me that I was to take the day off. He did not want me to think about work. He insisted, and before I knew it, I was out the door. That gesture was exactly what I needed. I will never forget how that act of kindness softened a very hard day for me. It allowed me to mourn my loss.

> "When you are kind to someone in trouble, you hope they'll remember and be kind to someone else. And it'll become like a wildfire."
> - Whoopi Goldberg

Full Circle

 t was a cold December day, and I needed a couple of things at the grocery store. Money was tight, and I had very little cash on me. As I got closer to the store, I noticed a woman ringing a bell and collecting donations for the Salvation Army. I felt guilty for walking by and not donating, but I was practically broke. I gave the woman a smile, and she smiled back at me.

I picked up my items, including a piping hot cup of soup from the take-out area. I was hungry, and I planned to eat the soup as soon as I got home. After I paid, I walked outside and heard that bell ringing. The woman had to be freezing. I reached into my bag, and pulled out the soup. "Do you like chicken noodle soup?" I asked. The look of gratitude on her face was priceless! Her reaction was ten times better than that soup would have been to me.

I will never forget the feeling that I had as I walked to my car. In the distance, across the parking lot, I faintly heard the woman yell, "God bless you!"

> *"Well something's lost but something's gained in living every day."*
> -Joni Mitchell, from *Both Sides Now*

I Could Take Him

I was at the grocery store and I was about to pay for my groceries. The checkout clerk was a demure 16-year-old girl. She smiled and seemed a little shy but she was very pleasant. An angry man came out of nowhere, screaming at this girl because *she* left his container of ice tea there. He was quite aggressive and he said that he was going to the manager and that she was going to be in big trouble. I was too stunned say anything to him and he stormed off before I could. I turned to the girl and she was trying so hard not to cry but the tears started flowing.

I told her that he was a raving lunatic and whatever his problem was it was not about her at all. I told her not to worry about him going to the manager - anyone could see him for what he was. I said that if she wanted I could go to the manager myself and explain what happened. I told her that if I ran into the man I'd kick his butt! I asked her if she thought I could take him. With that comment, she stopped crying and looked at me hard for a couple of seconds. She was trying to figure out if I was serious or not! We both started laughing, and I told her to forget all about him.

> "The most important thing for me is to know that I represent kindness. I'm glad I'm funny. I'm glad I make people happy, because that's very important. But I'm proud to be known as a kind person... Because kindness spreads and the world is a little nicer out there."
> - Ellen DeGeneres

Straight A's

My daughter left me a note telling me that she surprised some people that she did not know with kindness, and it made them happy. On my way to work, I stopped for gas and the owner of the gas station mentioned that he saw my daughter today. He wanted me to know that she is a very kind, respectful person, and how important that is in this day and age. I hear this a lot, and I am so proud of her. When others notice that my child is a thoughtful person, well, it is right up there with getting straight A's in my book!

> *"Being considerate of others will take your children further in life than any college degree."*
> - Marian Wright Edelman

Party Time

A new friend invited me to a party that he and his family were hosting. I sent an e-mail and I asked him what time the party was starting. His response was very sweet and it made me smile. He said, "I told everyone to come at five o'clock, but the party officially starts the moment you arrive!"

> *"A kind word is like a Spring day."*
> - Russian proverb

Down Under

I just started middle school and I was thrilled to find out that my club, People to People was traveling to Australia! We did a lot of fundraising, and we had to pay a portion of the expenses out of our own pockets, but we were all set to go. The person coordinating our trip told us that due to the price of fuel, the cost was increasing $1500 per person. My family was unable to contribute any more money for my trip. I was disappointed, but I understood. Where were we going to get that much money?

One Sunday I was walking out of church after the service. A man who is friends with my family greeted me, and he told me that he heard about my upcoming trip to Australia. I put my head down and I told him that I was not going this time. He said, "Yes you are, dear," and he handed me a check for $1500!

> *"There is nothing so rewarding as to make people realize that they are worthwhile in this world."*
> -Bob Anderson

One Good Deed Leads to Another

I had a flat tire and I pulled into the closest parking lot, which was a local fire station. I never changed a tire before, and I needed help putting on my spare. A man came out of the fire station and he offered to help me change it. When he finished changing my tire, I thanked him and I handed him a $20 bill. He refused to take it so I told him to donate the money to the fire company.

He smiled and this time he was thanking *me* for helping.

> *"We're here for a reason. I believe a bit of the reason is to throw little torches out to lead people through the dark."*
>
> -Whoopi Goldberg

Music To My Ears

A friend was telling me about her daughter's recent split with her boyfriend of several years. This young woman is a lovely girl. She has intelligence, personality, and beauty. Heartbreak can be devastating to anyone, and looking ahead is so difficult when the pain is here and now. I found my friend's daughter on Facebook and I sent her a message. I told her that I have been listening to a CD that she might relate to. The singer was going through a tough break up and the songs all dealt with her feelings about it. About a month later, my friend told me that her daughter is doing a lot better. Apparently, she discovered some music that was really helping her move on with her life.

> *"Music should go right through you, leave some of itself inside you, and take some of you with it when it leaves."*
>
> - Henry Threadgill

*B*ack in the early 1980's, my boyfriend and I took a spontaneous trip to Atlantic City. We arrived about 9:30 PM and managed to gamble until about 2:30 in the morning on our original cash. Five hours of gambling on $50 was unheard of! Then, we actually slept in his van on a local side street. We woke up later that morning and walked to the beach. We were hungry and had about three dollars between us. This was before the age of ATM cards, cash advances and cell phones. We did not have enough for breakfast and we hadn't even begun to think about the tolls. We were young and just not thinking things through.

We walked to the beach and started walking along the shoreline. It was so quiet compared to what the beach would be like in a couple of hours. I looked out at the ocean and it was taking my mind off our predicament. I started picking up shells and my boyfriend was skipping rocks. We splashed each other and I spotted a pretty scallop shell. As I bent down and put my hand in the water to grab it, a $20 bill wrapped around my wrist right in the water! I stood there and stared at it, then I picked it up and I was screaming in disbelief. I was jumping up and down, and my boyfriend was laughing at me and shaking his head. We looked at each other at the same time and we said, "Let's eat!"

> *"The universe conspires to be kind in your time of need."*
>
> - Barb Walters

I Believe

I am a social service director at a nursing home. My job is to be a liaison between the residents, their family, and the staff. It is important to make sure that the residents are comfortable and adjusting to living in this new setting. Many of the residents have senility and Alzheimer's disease, and some of the residents are here due to physical limitations.

When I make my rounds, I try to stop in and spend time with a patient named Mary. She is a very sweet elderly woman who has numerous physical limitations. Mentally, she is sharp as a tack. Sometimes it is hard to spend time with Mary, because she is so lonely. I want to spend more time with her, but I have to try to visit all of the patients. Mary likes to hold hands, and I remember, because I gently touched her hand one day, and she quickly put her other hand on top of mine and held it there. Recently, Mary casually told me that she prays for me every night. I did not really understand why she was praying for me, but she told me that she prays for me because she cares about me.

I could not really explain my reaction, because it surprised me. I got a lump in my throat, and I felt like I was going to cry. This sweet woman, with a list of painful physical ailments was not only thinking of me, she was praying for me. I know that there are scientific studies supporting the healing powers of prayer. I could not explain it, I did not understand it, but I did not have to. The fact that she prayed for me had a big impact on me. It really made me feel good. Mary was praying for me every night, and it brought me comfort. Thank you Mary! Your kindness made me believe in the power of prayer.

"There is no need for temples, no need for complicated philosophies. My brain and my heart are my temples; my philosophy is kindness."
-Dalai Lama

Hug

I was visiting my wife at her Assisted Living Facility. She has Alzheimer's disease, and she was not having a good day. As I was leaving, one of the workers stopped me. She told me that I looked like I needed a hug. She put her arms around me, and we hugged. That hug felt good. As I drove home, I realized something. I could not remember the last time anyone hugged me.

"Kindness is more than deeds. It is an attitude, an expression, a look, a touch. It is anything that lifts another person."
-C. Neil Strait

Dollar Signs

You know how some people find money? Coins and bills that are lying on the ground in a parking lot, the floor of a mall, or grocery store? My daughter is one of those people. She finds money a lot. One day when she was about ten, we were in a video store. The store was practically empty. I was scanning the shelves and she said to me, "Five dollars!" She picked up the bill lying on the floor right behind me. I sure didn't see it. She was staring at it with a big smile.

I heard something and I told my daughter to listen. It was a father talking to his young son at the front of the store. The boy was upset because he lost his five dollars and the dad was upset because he asked him to hold onto it and the boy did not. I looked at my daughter and smiled. I did not need to tell her what to do. She walked right over to them, and I heard the father who sounded quite surprised thanking my daughter for her honesty. The little boy was really happy too. My daughter came walking back down the aisle, and she was beaming with a huge smile on her face. I knew she learned something important. It feels really good to give back.

> "When you carry out acts of kindness you get a wonderful feeling inside. It is as though something inside your body responds and says, yes, this is how I ought to feel."
>
> -Harold Kushner

Old Glory

I t was the day after 9/11. We were all numb, scared, angry, and looking for ways to come together. The couple next door was away on a trip. He is a veteran and they have always had a flag up in their yard. I looked over at the flag and took my seven-year-old by the hand. I said there is something we had to do.

As we lowered the flag to half-staff, I explained that it was important as a symbol of respect and mourning. 'It'll be meaningful to our neighbors and anyone else who sees it.' When my neighbors returned from their trip, they called and thanked us, as they were hoping that we did just what we had done.

> "Kindness is a golden chain by which society is bound together." - Johann Wolfgang von Goethe

Coupons

I am a coupon clipper. When the coupons get close to expiring, I decide if I'll be using them. Sometimes I pull out the coupons that I won't be using, and I put them on top of that item in the grocery store. It takes a little effort but the idea of saving people money is so much better than throwing those coupons away!

> "Little kindnesses... will broaden your heart, and slowly you will habituate yourself to helping your fellow man in many ways."   - Zadik

Welcome

*P*lanning, organization, and practice saved 200 college girls in 1957 when we escaped the flames of our dormitory. A heavy snowstorm and dangerous winds broke a main wire. The broken wire created sparks which entered the closet in the old chapel. This ignited a fast-moving fire. When a student opened the door, flames and smoke burst into the room! All 200 girls escaped with only their pajamas, sneakers, a coat, and a flashlight. Our practice fire drills paid off, and all the girls cleared their dorms in less than two minutes! Attendance was checked at a building nearby, and every girl was accounted for. Word spread quickly and the story was on the national news and in the newspaper.

One of the girls had relatives nearby, and they drove through the snowstorm to pick us up. They took four of us into their home. There, we were able to phone our families. Those relatives even lent us their car to go to campus for classes. The faculty and community also came to our rescue. All the girls were provided with homes to stay in for the rest of the semester. The entire community welcomed us! The library, grocery store, and even the restaurants and bars stepped up, and they took us in too. It was amazing how everyone came through and supported us.

Planning, organization, and practice saved our lives, and we escaped the fire in 1957. Mostly, I will remember the people in the community who stepped up and welcomed us warmly, and without hesitation. They saved our spirit.

> *"None of us has gotten where we are solely by pulling ourselves up from our bootstraps. We got here because somebody bent down and helped us."*
> -Thurgood Marshall

When I heard the weed whacker out front, I looked out my dining room window expecting to see my husband. To my surprise, I saw a man working on our yard, but I had no idea who he was. He wore a hat and one of those allergy masks. I watched him as he edged along the street, and he trimmed around large rocks and flowerbeds. Then he moved down to my neighbors' yard, and he took care of their yard too. When he stopped at the next house, he took off his mask. That is when I realized that he lived there. We had spoken a couple of times in the past.

I walked over to his house, and I reintroduced myself. I thanked him for helping with my yard. He told me that whenever he works on his yard, he does the same for my neighbor and me. I smiled, and asked him why he does it. His response was simple, "Why not?"

> *"Of all the things I have learned in my lifetime, the one with the greatest value is that unexpected kindness is the most powerful, least costly, and most underrated agent of human change. Kindness that catches us by surprise brings out the best in our natures."*
>
> -Bob Kerrey

Coffee Break

I used to work the night shift at a mini-market. One night I was there alone, and I made coffee for the three separate machines. Each had a huge filter for coffee, and I filled the large pots with water and poured the water into each machine. Even at this late hour, people were still drinking a lot of coffee.

There was a lull in the store, and while I was standing by the cash register, I heard a very strange noise. It was a loud, pumping sound, and seemed to be coming from the coffee station. I walked over and one of the coffee machines was pulsating, with grounds shooting out the top and running down the sides of the machine. The unit was vibrating on top of the counter, and the hot coffee was overflowing and pouring over the top of the pot, running all over the counter. I must have poured two pots of water into the same unit by mistake!

I ran over and took the overflowing pot off the burner, and I put cups under where the coffee was pouring out. I tried grabbing napkins to sop it up but I did not have enough hands! Suddenly a man walked in. He was a regular and he always got a large coffee every time he came in. As soon as I saw him I cried, "Help me! " He ran over and we were both just trying to keep up with the overflow. It was so ridiculous that it became comical. A bunch of customers came into the store and I didn't know what to do. He told me to go ahead and take care of the customers. After the customers left, I went over to the coffee station, and remarkably, it was almost completely cleaned up. I thanked him profusely and I apologized for screaming at him. He said he was glad to help me.

The next time he was in the store, he brought his large coffee up to the cash register. He smiled and winked at me. Then he told me that I make really good coffee.

"Be the kind of person you would like to be with."
- Joseph W. Newton

Small Gesture

My neighbor's wife died suddenly. We were only acquaintances, but I heard that he was not doing well. I went over one day with a sympathy card and he invited me in. He was in bad shape. We really did not know each other, but I put my arm around him and told him that he was not alone. I let him know that I cared. I said that even though he doesn't want to, he should start eating and take better care of himself. I told him that every few days I would prepare him a meal, and I would bring it over and check on him. It seemed like such a small gesture but I've been told that it meant a lot to him. I saw him many times when he was at his lowest. Now we help each other out whenever we can.

"In about the same degree as you're helpful you will be happy."
- Karl Reiland

43

Pass It On

A young couple with two little girls used to be our neighbors. They moved but we still stay in touch. My husband and I look forward to an occasional phone call or letter. It is always a treat when the girls color pictures and send them to us. I had not heard from them in a while, so I gave them a call. I was saddened to hear my friend say that her husband quit his job in order to open his own business, and at the last minute, the deal fell through. Then, he was diagnosed with kidney cancer and had a kidney removed. He has a clean bill of health now, but she told me that it has been a very challenging and stressful few months. I got off the phone and talked to my husband about it. How much can one family take?

We wanted to help them, so we sent them a check. We received a call from them, and this time I spoke to my friend's husband. His first words to me were, "I don't know whether to thank you or to spank you!" We laughed, and I suggested he thank me. I was happy to hear that he found another job, and his health remains good. He told me that he really appreciates our help and he wanted to know what he could do to thank us. I told him that when he is in the position to help someone in need, he should simply pass it on.

> "No kind action ever stops with itself. One kind action leads to another. Good example is followed. A single act of kindness throws out roots in all directions, and the roots spring up and make new trees. The greatest work that kindness does to others is that it makes them kind themselves."
> - Amelia Earhart

44

We get a lot of takeout orders at the restaurant where I work. The customers come in, give me their name, pay me, and I give them their food. One night a woman came in and when she went to pay for her order, she discovered that she did not have her credit card with her, and she had no cash either. She seemed flustered and embarrassed. It was quite a large order, and I did not know what to do. I got my manager, and she came up front. She told the customer that she understood, and that she did not have to pay. Then she handed her the food. Naturally, the customer was very happy and grateful.

I was not sure if my manager performed this act of kindness because it was good for business, or if she did it out of the goodness of her heart. We never really talked about it. All I know is, I liked my manager before, but after I saw what she did for that woman, I liked her a lot more.

> "The key is to learn to respect and honor the complications of other people's lives."
> -Goldie Hawn

On the Road

I had just finished some errands and I was waiting at a light in the middle of a very busy intersection. A man on the corner was holding a sign. He had dreadlocks pulled back and there were tattoos on his face and neck. He wore a flannel shirt, cargo pants and boots, even though it was a hot summer day. I peered through all the cars to read his sign. It said, ON THE ROAD. OUT OF WORK AND HUNGRY. PLEASE GIVE IF YOU CAN. ANYTHING HELPS.

I saw someone give him something through their car window. I beeped and rolled down my window. He moved quickly, and before I knew it, he was standing by my door. As I handed him a five he looked right into my eyes and said, "Thank you, darlin." He was very thin. I was shocked that he was such a young man, maybe 25. When he went back to the corner the light changed. As I drove away, I noticed someone handing him a drink through their car window. I do not know what led him here, but he was down on his luck. It seemed like, at that moment anyway, his luck was changing.

> "I keep my ideals, because in spite of everything I
> still believe that people are really good at heart."
> - Anne Frank

Drive

a girl at my school is socially awkward, and she has trouble fitting in. She doesn't hang out with the in crowd, or wear the latest clothes. Since she doesn't have many friends, she spends a lot of time with her mom, and she is teased about it. I recently got my license, and I drive a used car my parents bought me. One day I was driving, and I saw them walking down the road. I stopped and I asked them if they wanted a ride. They happily accepted. They were both smiling ear to ear and they kept telling me over and over again how nice my car was. When I looked at them, I knew in my heart that their reaction had nothing to do with my car. They were just grateful that I stopped, acknowledged them, and picked them up.

> *"The time is always right to do what is right."*
> -Martin Luther King, Jr.

Gift Card

I was at the checkout line at a store, and a friendly couple was in front of me. The man smiled when he greeted me and asked me how I was. He paid with a gift card and as he was leaving, he handed the gift card to me so I could use the remaining balance on it. He told me to have a great day, and after that, I sure did!

> *"Don't wait for people to be friendly. Show them how."*
>
> -Author unknown

Love Thy Neighbor

*I*t was the first measurable snow of the season, and I needed to shovel a path for my dog. I got bundled up, and I opened the front door. Boy, was I surprised to find my neighbor snow-blowing my driveway. She had already cleared my sidewalk. I went back inside, and a few minutes later, she knocked on my door. I thanked her for her help and her concern for my safety. How lucky I am to have such a great neighbor!

> *"The best way to find yourself is to lose yourself in the service of others."*
>
> -Mahatma Gandhi

I work for a couple twice a month. Every time I am there, the woman gives me recipes or newspaper clippings that she has saved for me. Sometimes an article of clothing that she knows I would like, or a treat she picked up and wanted to share. I told her husband that his wife is one of the most thoughtful people I have ever known. Without missing a beat he said, "She is kind to every person she meets."

> *"You can gain more friends by being yourself than you can by putting up a front. You can gain more friends by building people up than you can by tearing them down. And you can gain more friends by taking a few minutes from each day to do something kind for someone, whether it is a friend or a complete stranger. What a difference one person can make!"*
>
> -Sasha Azevedo

Two Kind Strangers

I am an 81 year-old man and I went on a day trip with my AARP group. After the trip, the bus dropped us off at our vehicles. I was driving home thinking about the day. I was also thinking about my animals that were waiting for me, and I had a lot to do when I got home. My attention must not have been on the road, so when I took a turn I hit the curb. It was a bit of a shock. The car seemed fine at first but then it got shaky.

A young man in his 20's pulled up next to me and told me to pull over. Another car pulled up behind me with a man in his 50's. They did not know each other but they both wanted to be sure that I was okay. I was a little worked up but I was fine. The car itself was not damaged, but I did have one flat tire and another that was very low on air. The older man got out my jack and took off the flat tire and both men put on the spare and asked me how far I needed to go. Luckily, it was not far and they told me to drive slowly.

I thanked the men, two kind strangers, for their concern and assistance. I needed help and they had been there for me, which I greatly appreciated.

> "When I was young, I admired clever people.
> Now that I am old, I admire kind people."
> - Abraham Joshua Haskell

American People

I was returning home after grocery shopping with my two children, who are seven and four. As we rolled up the driveway, I realized I had forgotten my purse in the shopping cart, which I left in the corral in the parking lot! I quickly turned the car around and zoomed back to the store. The corral was empty of any carts with a purse, so I hustled the kids inside.

Luckily, at the service desk, there was my purse. Someone turned it in. Whew! On the way home, my daughter Allison remarked, "Mom, I think most people in America are good." I smiled and nodded with agreement at her surprising insight.

> "We are what we repeatedly do. Excellence then
> is not an act, but a habit."
>
> -Aristotle

Work Out

My friend and I started working out at the gym. My friend has long hair and a lot of it. She forgot to pull it back one day and she told me that it was going to be a mess to exercise with her hair in the way.

A very fit and tan woman must have heard us because she went to her backpack and returned with a hair tie for my friend. "Have a great workout!" she said.

> "No act of kindness, however small, is ever wasted."
> – Aesop, The Lion and the Mouse

Pen Pals

*E*very Christmas I send a card to an elderly woman that I have not seen since I was a teenager. She lived in my old neighborhood and she was friends with my parents. One day I had my address book open and I was addressing a thank you card. I noticed her name on the same page, and decided to send her a cheerful hello note.

She pleasantly responded and told me about her family. She seemed happy that she got my note. She even sent me pictures of her cats. I sent her a note back, and we have become pen pals. In this day and age, it is really special to give and receive kind notes in the mail.

> *"Remember there's no such thing as a small act of kindness. Every act creates a ripple with no logical end."*
>
> - Scott Adams

Strapped

*M*y wife and I were driving on a highway when we noticed that one of the straps holding down a load on the tractor-trailer in front of us flew off the truck. It landed on the side of the road. I used my CB radio to let the trucker know what happened. He asked me if I could pick up the strap for him since it would be easier for me than for him to turn his 18-wheeler around. I picked up the strap and we met up with the trucker at the next rest stop. We had coffee and talked, and he thanked us. Helping him to put that strap back on his load made traveling safer for him and others on the road.

> *"We cannot hold a torch to light another's path*
> *without brightening our own."*
>
> -Ben Sweetland

Roast Beef

$\mathcal{M}$any years ago, my neighbor had a baby. We were not close but we called ourselves friends. The day after she got home from the hospital, I brought over a roast beef dinner with heating instructions. That night she called me, and she sounded angry and annoyed. She told me that her husband insisted that she call. He wanted to know how I made the roast beef, because it was the best roast beef they had ever had. I could hear her husband in the background saying, 'Tell her yours tasted like bark off a tree!' We kind of laughed it off, but I knew his insensitive comment hurt.

My family moved out of the neighborhood and we lost touch, but I ran into her a couple months ago. The baby was all grown up and about to graduate from high school. I asked her how her husband was and she said that they divorced years ago. She paused, and with a sly smile she said, "I still make that roast beef though!"

> *"Food, like a loving touch or a glimpse of divine power, has that ability to comfort."*
> -Norman Kolpas

Bette's Roast Beef Recipe

3 to 4 lb. rump roast.
5 or 6 garlic cloves.
2 to 3 teaspoons of dry mustard.
One onion, cut in half.
Salt and pepper.
Preheat oven to 275°.

Tear off a large sheet of aluminum foil. Place roast beef on foil, make slits in the meat, and insert garlic cloves.

Sprinkle dry mustard over roast, and liberally use salt and pepper. Cut onion in half and put on top of roast.

Wrap up roast in foil. Tear another piece of foil and wrap roast again.

Place in a covered roasting pan to cook for four hours.

'Tis the Season

The holidays were approaching, and like most people in this country, I was stressed. There was work, shopping, money issues, decorating, wrapping etc. I felt very scattered. I had just finished what had to be my last trip to the grocery store before Christmas. I went all out and got prime rib, shrimp, scallops and all the delicious and most expensive items I could think of. I had so many groceries that I actually put some underneath my cart, which I never do. It was freezing cold and the wind was blowing as I put the groceries in my car. I wanted to just get home, put everything away, and collapse. I got home and as I put away the groceries, it seemed like I was missing some. I swear I had two or three more bags. Where were they?

I went back to my car and looked inside and in the trunk. Then it hit me. Those groceries were under my cart, which I returned to the cart rack. With a sinking feeling, I called the store right away and spoke to the manager. I told him what happened. He checked outside and at customer service. He informed me that my items were not returned and he wasn't very hopeful that they would be. I was disappointed but I was really embarrassed and upset with myself. The manager told me that he had an idea. He told me to circle all the missing items on my receipt and bring it into the store to show him. I did this at home and added them up with my calculator. It was $57 worth of missing items! I returned to the store with my receipt, found the manager, and told him I was the frantic woman on the phone. I thanked him for being so patient with me.

He looked at the receipt and gave it back to me. He told me to get a cart and replace every item I circled. He thanked me for shopping at the store and for being such a good customer. He wished me a happy holiday. It really *was* a happy holiday. His goodwill helped me get back into the spirit of the season.

> *"He who wishes to secure the good of others, has already secured his own."*
>
> -Confucius

Remembering

I am a chiropractor. One of my patients is a boy who is a great kid. His father is not in the picture at all. This boy never gets any presents or cards from his father for his birthday or Christmas. I feel terrible for the kid, and I make it a point to always remember him on those days. I give him a gift or a little cash because he deserves it. I know that it means a lot to him, and that means a lot to me.

> *"It's a great opportunity for all of us to raise the ante and the attention for something that needs focus. It's the cosmic food chain - that we get so much and we give something back - it's what we're supposed to do."*
>
> - Bonnie Raitt

Happy Birthday

I sure got a surprise for my 75th birthday. My wife and I joined three other couples at a restaurant for breakfast. They all sang happy birthday to me. A man approached our table, and he told us to come outside when we were finished breakfast.

We went outside and saw the man standing next to a beautiful motorcycle. He told me to get on the bike. Then he gathered everyone around me, and took our picture. He said he would get me a copy of the picture, and I told him where I lived.

I forgot all about it, and one day my wife and I were home watching TV. We heard a motorcycle and then there was a knock on the door. It was the same man we met at the restaurant. He handed me the picture of myself on his bike, surrounded by my wife and friends. I will always remember the lengths he went to make that birthday memorable.

> *"Those who bring sunshine to the lives of others*
> *cannot keep it from themselves."*
> - James Matthew Barrie

When my daughter was a teenager, she was best friends with a teenage boy. He was a great kid: funny, polite, respectful, and a real friend. His family had problems and his home life was troubled; he, his mother and his brother ended up living at a shelter.

I found out that his mom and brother could lose their place at the shelter, which is a scary thought. We offered to put him up at our house, but he had a curfew to follow, and had to sleep in the shelter until his mom found permanent housing. The shelter was clean, warm and provided food, but it was not a place you'd want to live in. It was heartbreaking.

This young man spent a lot of time with us, especially at dinnertime. The holidays were approaching and we were going to my in-laws on Christmas Eve. My daughter invited him to join us. We packed the car with the gifts we were exchanging. Their house was decorated beautifully for the holiday. The food was fabulous and the whole dinner was just lovely.

After dinner, we dispersed and had coffee and dessert. We decided to hand out our gifts. I handed him his gift bag and he opened his gifts. Afterwards, he came over, hugged me and thanked me. He was very grateful and I could tell that it meant a lot to him, but he was keeping his cool. A few minutes later, my dad pulled me aside and told me that he saw this kid looking at his gifts with tears running down his cheeks. I was touched when I heard that. I was happy that he had joined us, and it felt great to shine a little light on his holiday!

> *"There is no better exercise for your heart than*
> *reaching down and helping to lift someone up."*
> - Bernard Meltzer

Cheap Shot

My daughter was about to get her billiard lesson. She is not even a teenager yet but she is in a pool league of all men. She is a gifted pool player and the pool hall owner sometimes coaches a player who is willing to do the work and practice. While she was waiting for her lesson, she warmed up on another table. Her coach was finishing a lesson with a man who was in a wheelchair. I had seen him in there before, and as I watched him, I could see that he was really good. Pool is a lot harder than it looks. The position of your legs is important when you are shooting. He was doing it all with only his upper body. When his lesson was over, the man put his cue in his case. He started wheeling himself to the exit to leave. I walked over to the door, and I asked if I could get it for him. He thanked me but he told me that he had it. He opened the door and he wheeled himself to his van, which had a lift. I watched him, and I really admired him and his independence.

Suddenly I heard something that I could not believe. A kid who works there was making fun of this man. I was floored! I turned to him and told him that you could not get much lower than making fun of someone who is disabled. I told him how impressed I was with the man. I also pointed out that the man in the wheelchair shot pool a whole lot better than he did. I asked him if anyone ever taught him right from wrong. I told him that this is not a joking matter. Before I walked away, I said that he was very fortunate because he did not need a wheelchair, and for just one minute, imagine what life would be like if he did. I spoke on behalf of the man in the wheelchair, but I was desperately trying to teach this young man the importance of compassion.

"Kindness is the language that the deaf can hear and the blind can see."   - Mark Twain

60

*M*y son loves sports. He decided to collect sports equipment and donate it to charity. We figured that a good way to get the word out was posting on Facebook. To my surprise the one and only response I received was from a man serving in Iraq. He is the father of one of my son's friends. The man let us know that his family would go through their sports equipment and donate items to my son's cause. I was touched and honored that he took the time to support us. While serving our country in Iraq, he responded to *our* charity request here at home.

> "I am of the opinion that my life belongs to the whole community and as long as I live, it is my privilege to do for it whatever I can. I want to be thoroughly used up when I die. For the harder I work, the more I live. I rejoice in life for its own sake. Life is no 'brief candle' to me. It is a sort of splendid torch, which I have got hold of for the moment, and I want to make it burn as brightly as possible before handing it on to future generations."
>
> –George Bernard Shaw

The Red Shoes

I was entering kindergarten, and I was very excited about starting school. I knew the dress that I would wear, and the ribbon I wanted for my hair. I even got a new pair of shoes, red leather Mary Janes. I loved those shoes, and my mother said that they were really good shoes. One day a man from the Purple Heart was at our house. He was collecting donations of household goods. My mother was gathering up our belongings to donate, and I wanted to donate something too. I looked around my room, but my eyes keep going back to those new red shoes. I knew I would get in big trouble if I gave them away. I just kept thinking that I had other shoes to wear to school. Maybe a little girl did not have any shoes. Oh, how she would love these! I grabbed them, and I gave them to the man as he was turning to leave. He told me the shoes looked new, and he didn't want to take them. I think I said that they didn't fit, and with that, he was out the door.

After he left, I confessed to my mother. She flew out the door, and she ran down the street chasing that flat-bed Purple Heart truck. When the truck stopped, she climbed in the back. She was frantically searching for those shoes. As she pulled the shoes out of a large bag, my mother noticed a baffled friend stop her car by the truck. My mother explained why she was riffling through the truck. This friend just happened to work for the local newspaper. Even though my mother brought those red shoes home to me, my kind intention was headlined in the paper. The headline read, *A Good Little Citizen*.

> "No one has yet fully realized the wealth of sympathy,
> kindness, and generosity hidden in the soul of a
> child. The effort of every true education should be
> to unlock that treasure."   -Emma Goldman

Penny

It was the early 1960s. My buddy and I were out riding our bikes. It was really hot outside and we were dying of thirst. We stopped at a store and put our money together to buy a drink. We were a penny short, and we were so thirsty! We didn't know what to do. A nearby man reached into his pocket and gave us the penny so we could buy a drink.

Now, it sounds silly talking about a penny. On that day, fifty years ago, a penny meant a lot.

> "How beautiful a day can be when kindness touches it."
>
> -George Elliston

Change

I work at a local pizza parlor. One night, a woman came in with her young son, and she gave me her name, and said they were picking up their pizza. I had a feeling that they did not have a lot of money. I told her that her pizza cost $10.60. She took out a bag of change, and began to count it out on the counter. The little boy saw a picture of our bread sticks and dipping sauces, and he got excited, and told his mom that he wanted them too. She said, "Honey, mommy is going to be lucky if she has enough money for this pizza."

She counted out the $10.60, and she paid me. She had less than a dollar in change leftover, and put it in her pocket. I grabbed her pizza, along with an order of breadsticks, and handed them to her. She took the pizza and the breadsticks off the counter and she looked confused. As she was leaving the restaurant, she seemed uneasy and she glanced back at me. I smiled and told her to have a good night.

> "Be kind, for everyone you meet is fighting a hard battle."
>
> -Plato

Stop

I was riding in the car with my dad when we saw this car broken down on the side of the road, so we pulled over to check out the car. My dad is good with cars and he knew how to fix it. We turned around and drove to an auto parts store. We picked up the needed parts to return to the car. After a lot of time and effort, my dad fixed the car and then we were finally on our way. We spent over two hours helping that stuck driver. I asked my dad why he stopped and why he spent so much time helping. He told me that the driver needed the help. He hoped someone would stop what they were doing and help him if he ever needed assistance.

> "The purpose of life is not to be happy. It is to be useful, to be honorable, to be compassionate, to have it make some difference that you have lived and lived well."
>
> - Ralph Waldo Emerson

I Won

While honeymooning in Barbados we really wanted to experience the culture. We decided to frequent the spots the locals like. We came upon a little shack with a bar and slot machines. There was no air-conditioning, only ceiling fans. We ordered rum punch and it was not what we expected from punch. It was hot and spicy, kind of like the air in there. We started playing the slot machines. After a few minutes, a man who was playing a slot machine next to mine told me that I won.

He pointed to a little light that was lit on top of my machine. I did not understand. Where was my money? The man pointed to a button on my machine, and when I pushed it, money started pouring out of the machine. We were laughing and people were yelling. Money was spilling over the tray and onto the floor. We put all the coins in cups and cashed in. It looked like a lot more than it was, but $75 was a decent amount in those days. We took the money and left the shack.

In the distance, we heard reggae music, and we could see the glow of tiki torches. We walked up to a beautiful outdoor club playing live music. There were locals there along with vacationers. Everyone was dancing and having fun. We walked up to the bar and decided to buy everyone a drink with our winnings from the shack. We were treated like royalty! We met so many cool people, and we danced and partied all night long.

> *"That best portion of a good man's life: his little, nameless, unremembered acts of kindness and love."* — William Wordsworth

*O*ur house is surrounded by a lot of trees. Unfortunately, some of them are dying and they need to be cut down. We heard that a man in our neighborhood started a tree service business and he was very good. His family had gone through a lot of stressful events, and we were happy that his business was taking off.

We gave him a call and he and his son came over and took down many trees. They were efficient, cleaned everything up, and did a great job. When he handed me the bill I knew it couldn't be right. It looked like half the amount I was expecting. I asked if it included everything. He reminded me that a while back we helped his family out. I told him that it was not a big deal and besides it doesn't have anything to do with the tree removal. He smiled and said, "It does to me."

> *"It is one of the most beautiful compensations of this life that no man can sincerely try to help another without helping himself."*
> - Ralph Waldo Emerson

L-o-v-e

I returned to the animal shelter to adopt the white cat that our family decided on. When I walked back to her cage, I spotted a very scared-looking black cat with incredibly sad eyes. She looked like she needed a lot of love. The index card said that she was an adult cat, but she was tiny, maybe five pounds. I proceeded to the back of the shelter to pick up our white cat only to discover that she had already been adopted! This was a sign, and I knew that little black cat was destined to become a member of our family.

It is always a trick for cats to adjust to your family, and she was scared of everyone except me for a long time. She was an incredibly sensitive cat, and she seemed to read my emotions. When I sat on the sofa, she would reach over with her paw to touch my arm or try to touch my face. She would motion towards my face as if she's trying to let me know she was there for me, and she literally had a look of concern on her face when I was upset. This sweet, little black cat and I had quite a bond. She was the most caring animal I have ever known. I am lucky to have had such a wonderful friend.

> *"'How do you spell love?" Piglet asked Pooh.*
> *"I don't have to spell it," said Pooh. "I just feel it."'*
> \- A. A. Milne & E.H. Shepard

Gas to Spare

My wife and I were returning from a trip, and we stopped for gas. A family with two small children pulled up next to us, and they asked if we could spare any gas. The man said that they had car problems on their trip. They were out of money, and they still had an hour to go to get home. I really didn't know if they were being truthful. Whatever the reason was they needed help, so I put $10 of gas in their car when we were at the gas pumps.

> "Ask yourself: have you been kind today? Make kindness your daily modus operandi and change your world."
>
> > - Annie Lennox

Soup's On

I was sick with another sinus infection. I felt lousy and the medication was not helping. On top of feeling so terrible, I was very stressed with work. I was talking to a friend about how I just could not deal with it. A couple hours later, there was a knock on my door. It was my friend and she handed me a container of hot matzo ball soup. I don't know what made me feel better, that delicious soup or the fact that she made and delivered it to me!

> "The everyday kindness of the back roads more than makes up for the acts of greed in the headlines."
>
> > - On the Road with Charles Kuralt

Unforgettable

I was in the kitchen when I heard the crash. I ran outside and realized that a bread truck had struck a boy on his bike. The impact was so forceful that it blew his sneakers right off his feet. I stood there staring at him lying in the street, when suddenly he leapt into my arms. He was hugging me and holding on for dear life.

I called to my daughter and asked her if she knew this boy and where he lives. She pointed down the street. I ran down the street with him in my arms and found his house. I handed him to his mother and suggested she take him to the hospital.

Many years later, I was making a purchase at an electronics store. The salesperson asked me if I knew him. I could not place him. He told me that he could never forget the woman who carried him home after he was hit by the truck. It turned out that he had been injured, but he is fine now. He thanked me for comforting him and bringing him home.

> "I don't know what your destiny will be, but one thing I know: the only ones among you who will be really happy are those who will have sought and found how to serve."
> - Albert Schweitzer

Lucky Dog

I am a widower and my pets are my responsibility and are my family. My vet told me that one of my cats had fleas, even though they never go outside. I was treating my dog monthly with flea medicine, so I didn't get it. I decided to buy flea medicine for all my pets, and I gave them all their doses. I sprayed the whole house for fleas. This was getting quite expensive and frustrating. My dog was still scratching, even after the flea medicine. I felt like I was having a streak of bad luck. My neighbor is a dog groomer and she came over to trim my dog's nails. I told her about the flea issue and my dog scratching.

She examined my dog, and found dermatitis, but no evidence of fleas. She wanted to give the dog a bath every ten days with a special shampoo until her problem cleared up. We could do this at my house. She also suggested a high-protein dog food, and she gave me a few cans to try. I was thrilled that my dog didn't have fleas, and it sounded like there could be a solution to the scratching. I was happy and I knew that my dog would be happy too. I asked the groomer if she could give me an estimate of the cost. She told me that she was not charging me and refused to take any payment at all.

> *"Kindness is the only service that will stand the storm of life and not wash out. It will wear well and will be remembered long after the prism of politeness or the complexion of courtesy has faded away."* - Abraham Lincoln

Breaking In

My wife was away for the weekend. I was taking care of our five-year-old son, who was sick with a fever. Neither of us slept well, and I was edgy. Midmorning, I must have been nodding off, but I was jolted awake by a very loud bang. It was so loud, that it sounded like a dresser fell over. I checked my house and nothing seemed out of place. My neighbor on the other half of our townhouse lives alone. He is in good health, but he is elderly. His dog had not stopped barking since that loud bang. I was getting worried. I told my son to stay put, and I went next-door and pounded on his door to make sure he was okay. There was no answer, and the dog was barking like crazy. I knocked on the other neighbors' doors, but nobody knew where he was, and nobody had a key to get in.

Now, I am a pretty big guy and I was losing my cool a little. My neighbors were getting concerned too. I got my credit card out and tried to unlock his door. I fooled around with it for a while, and when I turned the handle, the door opened. It was like in the movies, although I don't think the lock was completely latched, but I was in! The dog was barking, but she calmed down when she recognized me. I was calling for my neighbor and looking around. Nothing was amiss and the house was as neat as a pin.

Then I looked at the basement door, which was opened halfway. I was afraid to look down the steps, but I did look. I was relieved he was not lying at the bottom. Finally, I checked the garage, and his car was gone. I knew that he was all right, so I went back home.

When my neighbor got home, I went over and told him that there was a lot of commotion when he was gone. I apologized for breaking into his house, but I was concerned that something happened to him. He thanked me and he was touched that I went to such lengths to check on him. We were both completely stumped about the loud bang.

When my wife got home, I was embarrassed. I told her what happened. Within minutes, she informed me that the ceiling fan fell out of the third-floor window. She went right over to tell our neighbor. She apologized again for me breaking in, and my neighbor was smiling. He kept telling my wife that he was grateful and he was glad that the mystery was finally solved. Then he handed her his spare key… just in case.

> *"You cannot do a kindness too soon for you never know how soon it will be too late."*
> -Ralph Waldo Emerson

In My Hands

*O*ur orange, male, tabby cat passed away, and we wanted to get a kitten, preferably an orange male. We found the perfect orange kitty at a pet store near our home. He was adorable, playful, and he loved to cuddle up in your lap. We were about to sign the papers to adopt him, when I remembered a friend of mine who had ten stray cats that she took care of in her garage. She was always looking for homes for them, so I decided to give her a call.

She thought the best cat for us was this funny-looking black and brown adult male cat. He has big ears, a thin coat, and a stumpy tail. She told me that he wandered into her garage about eight months ago, and he was starving. She described him as a loving cat who desperately wants to be an inside cat, and he tries to get inside her house every day. My daughter, her friend, and I went over to meet him. We entered the garage, and all the cats scattered and hid, or they tried to escape through a window. My friend managed to grab the cat she told us about, and we all went inside the house.

She placed him on my lap and he was trembling. His right eye was squinting, his nose was running, and he flinched every time there was a strange noise. I could tell that he was trying to be still, and he kept looking at my friend for reassurance. We all petted him, and my daughter and her friend left after a few minutes. My friend told me that she would have him tested to make sure he was healthy, and let me know the results. I sat there holding and petting this shaking cat, and even though he was scared, he was purring. He just needed some love. I felt like his future was in my hands. This could be his only chance to have a real home, since most people do not want adult cats. I told my friend that I would have to talk to my family, but we would probably take him. When I got home, my daughter told me that she really wanted that adorable orange kitten. I explained the reasons why we should take the adult cat, and how sweet and loving he was. She agreed that it was the right thing to do, although he was not exactly what we were looking for.

We ended up adopting that funny-looking misfit cat. We are positive that we made the right decision by picking him, and he is one of the coolest cats we ever had. He is now a distinguished looking cat, with lots of charisma. Mostly, he is loving, and grateful. He has filled the void in our lives, and added something special with his loving ways. He is now receiving the attention he has craved for so long. He reminds me every day that adult animals make great pets, and they need a chance. When you adopt a pet in trouble, you change their life forever. They will change your life too, with their love and gratitude.

> *"There are no random acts. We are all connected.*
> *You can no more separate one life from another*
> *than you can separate a breeze from the wind."*
> -Mitch Albom, from *The Five*
> *People You Meet in Heaven*

You Came Back

I live in an upper middle-class neighborhood, with finely manicured lawns and large properties. I was going to the grocery store, and I noticed a woman sitting at the edge of a lawn by the street. It was a very hot day, but she was wearing jeans. She was just sitting there by the road, and it was odd. I went to the store and I looked for the woman on my way home. Now she was lying on the ground in such a position I thought she was in distress. I parked the car and went over to her. She sat up, and I asked her if she was all right. I wanted to help her. She said that she used to live in the neighborhood and she wanted to try to break into her old house to look for food. I asked her when she last ate, and she shrugged. She told me that she had some water yesterday. I wanted to take her somewhere to get her some food, but she refused. She kept saying that gas was too expensive. She told me that she was waiting for her boyfriend who was trying to get them a spot at a campground. She insisted that she was fine, and I left.

I drove home and put my groceries away, but I could not let this go. I grabbed a cold soda, and I went back. I parked my car, and I walked over to her. As I handed her the soda, she kept saying, "I can't believe you came back!" I told her that I wanted to take her to her boyfriend. When I offered to drive her, she kept telling me that it was too much, but I insisted, and she finally gave in. She grabbed two tattered backpacks that were hidden under some bushes. She said that everything she owned was in those bags. I looked at those worn backpacks, and I just could not imagine being in her shoes.

When we were driving to the campground, she commented that no one else even acknowledged that she was sitting there by the road. She could not believe that I came back, and now

I was driving her to where she needed to go. I kept telling her that it wasn't a big deal, and it wasn't. She hugged me when we arrived at the campground. I handed her $10 and insisted she get something to eat. As I watched her walk away, I knew that what I did meant a lot to her. What I did not expect was that it meant a lot to me too.

> *"Too often we underestimate the power of a touch,*
> *a smile, a kind word, a listening ear and honest*
> *compliment or the smallest act of caring, all of*
> *which have the potential to turn a life around."*
> -Leo Buscaglia

Two-For-One

My son was about to turn 18 and he planned on going to the shore for a couple of days. I wanted to get him emergency road service coverage in case he had any car trouble. I found an auto service club to join and they quoted a flat rate for him. It would be another $50 to add a second driver. Money was tight, so I decided just to get him covered for now.

A couple of hours later, the woman I spoke to called me back. She originally had not noticed my son's age. She suggested that I put the membership in my name instead. This way I would have coverage, and my son could have free coverage until he was 19. Now we both have emergency road service coverage, and I did not have to pay the extra $50. I was happy to get the added coverage, but what really impressed me was the fact that the woman called me back and assisted me. It made my day.

> *"By doing simple acts of kindness for others, we can't help but lift ourselves up, too."*
> -Source Unknown

After a snowstorm, I got a call from a friend. Her neighbor's mother lives in my neighborhood and apparently, the person who shovels her walk and sidewalk wasn't around. My friend asked if my husband and I would help her. We walked down the street and I knocked on her door to let her know who we were and what we were doing. She tried to pay us but we didn't want any money.

As we finished shoveling, my husband noticed an elderly woman in the street trying to get to her car. We both walked over and started helping her and digging her car out. It turned out that her husband was in the hospital and she wanted to go visit him as soon as she could. We were happy to help. What a wonderful way to meet two of our neighbors!

> *"To know even one life has breathed easier because*
> *you have lived, this is to have succeeded."*
> -Ralph Waldo Emerson

Laundry Day

The family down the street had been struggling for a while, since their teenage son had major health issues. They were up to their necks in bills. They were just trying to survive in this terrible economy. We did not know them but we reached out to them and wanted to help.

I spoke with the mother, she vented about her child's health, their bills, and how she felt like her life was unraveling. She said on top of everything else, her dryer stopped working and her washer did not spin anymore. It had been raining for days, they had muddy towels from their dogs, and they could not wash them. They were also down to one working vehicle, which was used for work and doctor appointments, so it was hard to get to the Laundromat.

I looked in the newspaper for a couple weeks for a used washer- dryer. I found an ad in the paper with a great price for both, and my husband and I went to the house to check it out. They were spotless and practically new. The couple said their daughter had severe allergies and they were getting a special washer-dryer that was being delivered that day. It was a great deal, so we paid them, and then returned with a truck. A friend helped load them and deliver them. The family was happy and it was wonderful to find some way to make their life a little easier.

> "A gift consists not in what is done or given, but
> in the intention of the giver or doer."
>
> -Seneca

My mom and I were helpers at a Relay for Life fundraiser. A group of us had a table set up in front of a large store and we were selling baked goods. I was not quite a teenager yet and I was at that awkward stage. I was self-conscious about my appearance and I was very shy. I said hello to everyone in the group but that was it. My mom said something funny and I laughed. One of the men in our group looked at me and said, "You know you're really pretty when you smile." It really made me feel good to get a compliment like that, especially since it was from someone other than my mom.

> *"People, even more than things have to be restored, renewed, revived, reclaimed and redeemed. Remember, if you ever need a helping hand, you'll find one at the end of your arm. As you grow older, you'll discover that you have two hands. One for helping yourself, the second for helping others."*
> -Sam Levenson, from *Time Tested Beauty Tips*, referenced by Audrey Hepburn

Young at Heart

I love pop-up books; I have ever since I was a child. The construction, the planning, the designs and imagery come together in a remarkable way. Pop-up books are always filled with surprises. I recently received a wonderful gift from my sister-in-law. Initially I thought it was a large colorful book about birds. We are both bird lovers and I was looking forward to reading the book. I opened the book and to my surprise, it was a pop-up book with sounds of birds in their natural habitat.

When I paged through the book I delighted in all of the talent and imagination at work. I smiled as I turned each page. It reminded me of the wonders of childhood. Curiosity and imagination are piqued and you become excited about all the possibilities of the world. That is the feeling I never want to outgrow.

> *"Dig within. Within is the wellspring of Good;*
> *and it is always ready to bubble up, if you just dig."*
> - Marcus Aurelius (2nd century A.D.)

We all have it inside ourselves to be kind to one another. Random acts of kindness bring out the best in people. They have a way of giving us confidence and a new gratitude for life. Even very small acts of kindness are important in our daily routines, and small actions have a way of making a big difference to others. Our world needs kindness now more than ever. The recession is making people realize that materialism and fortune may not be the answer for our happiness. Think back and remember acts of kindness that you have experienced. Were you the giver or the receiver? Those memories keep an emotional picture of that event with an image that is more valuable than material possessions. We need to realize that random acts of kindness come into our lives often, and in many creative forms. A beautiful work of art, a moving piece of music, or any wonder of nature. Something as simple as a smile on a child's face, or a hug. These are all acts of kindness. If we become more aware of the goodness in our lives, we will be grateful for what we already have.

Find something that you have to offer: a kind word, support for a friend who is down or a cooked meal for someone who is alone. Use your imagination, but do something! Find ways to be kind, and you will make a difference. You will also encourage others to do the same. Just try it and you will see. When you look for and find ways to help others, your world gets bigger, and kindness always seems to find its way back to you. It just does. Since kindness is reciprocated on a smaller scale, wouldn't it be great if the world could rethink how its problems are addressed? Kindness could be that special ingredient that makes us come together to live peacefully and prosper. Maybe I'm a dreamer, but what a wonderful, positive idea for us all!

I am very grateful that I have learned a lot about kindness, and about life, from very important teachers: my family, friends, people I have worked with, and random strangers who reached out to me in some way. I have learned so much, and I am so very grateful to everyone who not only passed their stories along, but who continue to take just a little time to be kind and to help others in some way. One of my favorite quotes relates to serving others and it is a true lesson in life:

> *"The easiest way to get what you want is to help others get what they want."*
>
> -Deepak Chopra

In my heart, I know that what we all want, what we need more of in this life... is kindness.

About the Author

Barb Walters has worked as a social service director, teen counselor, and medical office manager. She currently helps others through her cleaning and pet-sitting business. She enjoys cooking (a former Pillsbury Bakeoff finalist), listening to  music, and writing. She lives in Pennsylvania with her husband, daughter, and two cats.

Made in the USA
Lexington, KY
23 April 2014